CLOSING ARGUMENTS

poems by

Lori Shpunt

Finishing Line Press
Georgetown, Kentucky

CLOSING ARGUMENTS

Copyright © 2016 by Lori Shpunt
ISBN 978-1-944251-58-1 First Edition
All rights reserved under International and Pan-American Copyright Conventions.
No part of this book may be reproduced in any manner whatsoever without written permission from the publisher, except in the case of brief quotations embodied in critical articles and reviews.

ACKNOWLEDGMENTS

Earlier versions of Naming the Animals and God's Regrets appeared in the chapbook *Escape Routes* (Pudding House Press).
An earlier version of The Difference Between Men and Women appeared in the chapbook *Moving Expenses* (Still Waters Press).

Editor: Christen Kincaid

Cover Art: Lori Shpunt

Author Photo: Rick Cannon

Cover Design: Elizabeth Maines

Printed in the USA on acid-free paper.
Order online: www.finishinglinepress.com
also available on amazon.com

Author inquiries and mail orders:
Finishing Line Press
P. O. Box 1626
Georgetown, Kentucky 40324
U. S. A.

Table of Contents

In the Beginning 1

Knowledge 2

The Explanation 3

Losing Eden 4

The Trick 5

The Serpent Speaks 6

Afterwards 7

Dominion 8

Weapons 9

Apple 10

Naming the Animals 11

The Difference between Men and Women 13

The First Night 14

The Defense 15

God's Regret 16

The Way It Really Happened 17

for the women in my corner—
Linda, Theresa, Sue, Saundra, Sondra

IN THE BEGINNING

Overhead, a thin moon gleams.
The harsh calls of night birds pierce a marbled navy sky.
In this black perfume of blooming flowers,
anything can happen,
anything can happen
in the dark.

Now the garden is ready.
The players are stirring,
about to waken.
And see, over there, the yellow unlidded eyes glow.
The snake's pink tongue flickers,
and he uses his horned head
to part the leaves of a tree
bent low with red apples.

There.
He sees her.
The overture has ended.

Eve,
she enters, stage left.

KNOWLEDGE

The snake slid away, hid in the dangerous tree.
And after the gate banged shut
we waited.
We could still taste
the apple in our teeth.

We waited scared
and excited to learn
what the snake had promised,
what we'd been forbidden to know.

But night arrived with the same full sky
of bright stars shining.
Nothing at all had changed.

He said it first:
Maybe the snake lied.
Maybe we already know everything.

But then he turned and saw me in the moonlight.
His eyes slid over my naked body
leaving a trail of heat.

Shame spread through me like a stain.
And as I reached for leaves to cover myself,
a new desire bloomed inside me.

This is what I wanted to know.

I let the plucked leaves fall.

THE EXPLANATION

Adam went crazy
right after it happened,
grieving for Eden,
trying to find a way back in.
But it was over.

He blamed me:
Your mistake! Your mistake!
Whole days he'd pace
and scream: *A piece of fruit?*
He seemed to forget
that he ate the apple, too.
I didn't speak.
I let him rant.
It calmed him.

And now years later,
there are still times
when the young boys point at me and say it:
"She's the one. She let a snake play her."

Maybe. But when women
ask me why I did it, when they ask about the snake,
I tell them and they just nod—

The snake listened to me.
I talked to him,
and he listened.

LOSING EDEN

Everyone wants to hear about before—
the good stories: the shaped clay, the stolen rib spinning into flesh,
a garden's glory.

How could I let it go?

Sometimes I just lie:
the terrible serpent, the shine of the red apple skin.

But the truth is
the garden was a drag.
Every day was the same:
the endless sky, a bright blue bubble;
the wind, a whisper, lullaby breeze.

And in the center of it all—
a tree we couldn't touch.

I got tired of the tease.
And I wanted that fruit.
I wanted to know what He knew
and wouldn't tell us.

Escape, the snake whispered.
Yes, I said. *Yes.*

THE TRICK

Outside Eden we waited,
our limbs
turning numb with the cold.
It was over so quickly:
the apple eaten,
the serpent gone.
Now what?

Sorrow rolled in,
surrounded us like fog.
We both began to shiver.

I'm sorry, I whispered.

I don't know how long we sat
asking forgiveness, screaming for help.
Days, months, years.
It didn't matter.

He'd known from the start we'd fail.

THE SERPENT SPEAKS

Eve liked secrets
right from the beginning—

So I showed her how the sunlit lake
could be a mirror
and waited for her to get hooked.

She'd wade through the weeds
to get to unclouded water.
She'd watch
her face for hours
in every kind of light.

The afternoon light, she told me,
shows off my better side.

But I could see right away
she was dissatisfied.

Listen, I said, *the apple can change you—*
highlight your face,
halo your hair,
smooth out the lines in your skin.

In seconds, she decided
and grew,
with each bite,
more beautiful to me.

AFTERWARDS

1
A cold rain began,
the drops so large
they hurt the skin.
And the mosquitoes appeared,
landed, drew blood.
The sky darkened.

This is what you wanted,
he yelled, shivering
in the crumpled leaves.

2
Well, I said,
the rain will probably end.
And it did.
And the mosquito welts faded;
the itching stopped.

The sun came back,
warming us.
Our raw and naked skin throbbed.
And we looked at each other
no longer perfect

but still
somehow
designed for love.

DOMINION

He loved it at first.
I'd watch him: in charge,
the boss of everything that moved.
The ground creatures with scales,
the furred, the clawed—
all crawled to his orders.
A whole sky of birds
landed and flew to his voice.

Sometimes, he'd show off—
make the fox float,
insist the lions swim,
on and on.
He told me, too,
what to do, where to go.
And I went along.
For a while, I smiled and
obeyed him, but I was waiting
to make my own way
in the garden.

And when the snake appeared,
promising to reveal
the evil and good the heart held,
I told him
I already know. I already know
about power and wanting it.

Show me, he said.
Get him to eat this apple.

WEAPONS

The angels made us leave
and suddenly the animals, too,
turned on us, all claws and snarling,
eyes red, yellow with rage.

We ran, hid, blood racing through our chests,
trying to map the new landscape,
trying to survive.

So we did what God did.
We made a sword.
We set it on fire.
We shouted *AWAY*
swinging the burning blade.

And we built our own fence, locking out
what we feared,
whatever could hurt us,
whatever no longer obeyed.

APPLE

There were sweeter pieces of fruit in the garden—
kiwi, mango, peach.
There were pieces easier to reach,
easier to peel.

Apple, the snake said.
This tree.
This fruit.

The glossy red skin is tight against my teeth,
cracks to crisp, white pulp underneath.
And before I can swallow,
the snake escapes.

The hard apples melt and wrinkle to char.
The bent tree blazes into flame.
Black leaves burn along snapping branches,

and the air is suddenly sour
with a new rotting smell.

Fear. This is its day.
This is its odor.
This is the new day dawned.

NAMING THE ANIMALS

Adam found it easy, stayed
with one syllable words:
cow, mink, frog.
He pointed once
at each creature and spoke:
newt, jay, fox.

No, Eve said. *That's too quick.
You're missing the complexity.*

When it was her turn
she took time, considered everything—
the animal's look and texture,
the way the tendons moved,
the noises it made at the moon.
Listen: rhinoceros, giraffe, ocelot.

Finally, he complained.
*At this rate, we'll never finish.
Why are you making it so difficult?
Life is so easy.*

Now it's easy, she said. *But what if things change?*

Change? Why would anything change? he asked
as he held up the next creature—
thick, scaled, wriggling.
Snake, he said.

No, she said. *I don't think so.*
That's not the right name:
it's something more complicated, something dangerous
and different...

and she tried to back away from
the split hissing tongue.

THE DIFFERENCE BETWEEN MEN AND WOMEN

In the beginning
The garden grows a hundred shades of green,
lush in the sunlight: easy, easy.
She hums
in the glow of the moon, crushing blossoms.
He sleeps, sleeps, sleeps
chasing dreams.

I want to know everything about you,
she says in the morning,
dark eyes shining, open as sky.
So he tells her
everything he knows and
everything he wants, and
slowly unfolds his hidden heart.

She tries to sleep.
Jasmine and lilies garland the air.
Her full, red heart opens, closes.
She turns and finally asks him.
You don't want to know everything about me, do you?

No, he says, *no.*

And the green gate closed,
and the rain erupted,
and the ripe fruit rotted in his hand.

THE FIRST NIGHT

Trapped in the dark
we thought
the light had left
forever.

We stopped what we were doing.
We closed our useless eyes.

How can we live in the dark?
We can't see anything.

I listen to him breathe, breathe, breathe.

Finally he whispers:
Light isn't everything.
We'll learn to do without it.

The small night noises thrash in our ears.
The odors of animals find us.

We reach for each other.
We'll trust just our skin.
And whatever we touch
is all that there is.

THE DEFENSE

1
After the strange snake spoke,
after the sky roared open,
after an angel on fire swept us away and sealed the gate,

we lay in terror, silent.

2
The mud dark night filled with noises we'd never heard before.
We screamed,
we pounded our fists on the gate.
We begged and shouted,
collapsed into sleep.

3
In the morning, we made a list of our questions.

Why did you make the snake?
Why did you tell the snake about the tree?
Why did you test us?
Did you know we would fail?
Why were we the only flaw in your creation?

GOD'S REGRET

How did it all go wrong?
It should have been so easy.

Avoid the tree.
That's all I said.

Then I set them free in the garden.
I trusted them.

Sometimes I look at the scrapbook of Eden.
Slowly, I flip through the pages of pictures:
Adam laughing in the sunlight,
Eve's gentle face smiling,
blurred against a backdrop of lilies,
all of it already
beginning to fade.

THE WAY IT REALLY HAPPENED

In Eden
everything was all it ought to be.
There was no need
to need anything.
You see how it was.

Your turn to bite, I said.
Teeth snap down,
cold to the core,
and the apple is gone.

So I tell him the truth:
I knew what would happen.
I was bored.

Lori Shpunt has retired as *Professor Emerita* of English from Trinity College in Washington, DC, where she taught courses in poetry, film, and women's studies for 40 years. She earned her M.F.A. and Ph.D. at the University of Iowa.

Her first chapbook, *Moving Expenses*, was published in 2000 by Still Waters Press after winning the Women's Words Competition. Her second chapbook, *Escape Routes*, was published in 2007 by Pudding House Press. She has twice been selected for Individual Artist Awards in Poetry—in 2000 and 2003—by the Maryland State Arts Council. In 2000, she delivered a series of lectures on contemporary American poetry at the Smithsonian entitled "Unlocking Modern Poetry."

Her poems have appeared in *Louisiana Literature, The Comstock Review, Sojourner, Peregrine, Whole Notes, Cumberland, Poetry Review, Poetpourri, The Aurorean.* From Silver Spring, Maryland, she and her husband of 45 years, poet Rick Cannon, have five grown children and seven grandchildren. She reads mysteries and loves all kinds of puzzles. She is currently working on a book about her family.

www.ingramcontent.com/pod-product-compliance
Lightning Source LLC
Chambersburg PA
CBHW060227050426
42446CB00013B/3215